RYA Safety Boat Handbook

by Laurence West and Grahame Forshaw

Edited by David Ritchie

Illustrator: Pete Galvin

2007

© RYA 2007

First Published 2007

The Royal Yachting Association

RYA House, Ensign Way, Hamble

Southampton SO31 4YA

Tel: 0845 345 0400

Fax: 0845 345 0329

Email: publications@rya.org.uk

Web: www.rya.org.uk

ISBN: 978-1-905104-383

RYA Order Code: G16

Totally Chlorine Free   **Sustainable Forests**

A CIP record of this book is available from the British Library

Note: While all reasonable care has been taken in the preparation of this book, the publisher takes no responsibility for the use of the methods or products or contracts described in the book.

Cover design: Balley Design Limited

Photographic credits: Grahame Forshaw, Laurence West, Gingerpix and David Ritchie

Thanks also to Minorca Sailing, Thorney Island Watersports Centre and CYE Sailing Centre

Video Photography: Laurence West, Grahame Forshaw edited by Paradigm Design.

Typeset: Creativebyte

Proofreading and index: Alan Thatcher

Printed in China through World Print

All prices shown are correct at the date of publication.

Safety Boat Handbook

Foreword by James Stevens
TRAINING MANAGER AND CHIEF EXAMINER

RYA courses teach self reliance. Sailors and powerboaters should take to the water with the intention of returning without assistance. However for sailing schools, beginners, children, and during races it is important that there is safety cover provided by a powerboat.

It is equally important that the helmsmen of these safety boats are knowledgeable and trained. At an RYA recognised centre or affiliated club competitors or trainees can expect a competent safety boat coxswain who will have positioned the safety boat in the right place, know the priority of rescuing people before boats, and know how to cope even if the rescued crew are unable to assist. Steering a powerboat is a simple skill but manoeuvring a safety boat around a capsized dinghy with sailors in the water and ropes just under the surface requires considerable skill.
As new types of boats and equipment are introduced, techniques of rescue have to change. The RYA, keen to encourage the new generation of dinghies, leads the world in providing advice to safety boat crews and has researched the difficulties caused when these craft invert following a capsize. Advice to safety boats is included in these pages and has been drawn on by the International Sailing Federation (ISAF) and the RNLI.

This book is a compilation of many years experience as well as recent research. Its authors Grahame Forshaw, Laurence West and David Ritchie each have a lifetime's experience as safety boat coxswains and instructors. They bring pragmatism and good sense to the subject and provide an invaluable reference to sailing schools, clubs and any other organisation providing safety cover to small craft.

Safety Boat Handbook

THIS SYMBOL APPEARS THROUGHOUT THE BOOK AND DENOTES THAT MORE INFORMATION IS AVAILABLE ON THE ACCOMPANYING DVD.

Introduction by David Ritchie
NATIONAL SAILING COACH

The book is laid out in a logical order, recognising that the basic skills and principles involved in recovering different craft must be mastered before moving on to more complex situations such as inversions.

It starts with some quick reference check lists to remind you of the basics as required.

Most sailors, windsurfers and other water users will be able to sort themselves out following an incident, but the situations in this book assume some assistance is required. The attached DVD is designed to provide you with demonstrations of some of the many different ways of recovering personnel and equipment. For the purpose of clarity and simplicity only, the sequences generally involve solo operators and craft with no crew.

There are sections on giving assistance in a wide range of situations, in recognition of the fact that safety boat crew sometimes encounter water users beyond their immediate brief or that of the RYA as the governing body for windsurfing, sailing and powerboating.

Acknowledgements

The RYA is grateful to the BKSA and BCU for their comments in the preparation of the book, and to the large number of sailors, instructors and drivers who have contributed, too many to mention by name.

Check and tidy equipment. Coil lines, secure fuel tanks and secure or stow loose equipment – a tidy boat is a safe and effective boat.

Attach the kill cord before starting the engine.

After starting the engine, check for the cooling water tell-tale, check the steering has free and easy movement across the full range. Check the kill cord is working.

- Before manoeuvring, communicate your intentions to the crew, or anyone else in the boat e.g. "Power on and turning left" or simply "Hold on".

- Apply 'Brain – Steering – Throttle' for the most precise manoeuvre in an outboard powered boat.

- When manoeuvring near other craft, observe the rules of the road.

- Be aware of the tide and changing weather conditions.

- When driving at planing speeds in particular, keep a very good lookout.

- Communicating can be difficult, so consider turning off the engine to talk to another crew.

Upon approaching a capsized craft, count heads and take great care. Ensure that both the crew receiving assistance and the safety boat crew are aware of your intentions before acting.

You can prevent boats from inverting by holding the mast tip or the forestay.

With someone in the water, stay in the helmsman's seat between the casualty and your propeller. Once in contact turn off the engine unless there is a compelling reason not to e.g. a very close lee shore.

Take care lifting people from the water – do not injure yourself.

If you are going to engage in a tow, prepare the boat before passing any lines.

Safety Boat Handbook

RIGHTING A BOAT: GUIDING PRINCIPLES

Think about wind direction and count heads as you approach a capsized craft. If more than minor assistance is required, recover the crew before dealing with the boat.

Dinghies

If working from the hull side, position the rig pointing downwind, so that as the boat comes up, the sails blow away from you.

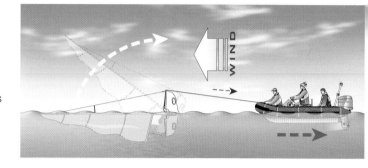

If lifting the mast, position the rig pointing upwind. The sails will blow away from you once righted.

Multihulls

Use the wind under the rig to assist in righting – rig upwind of hull.

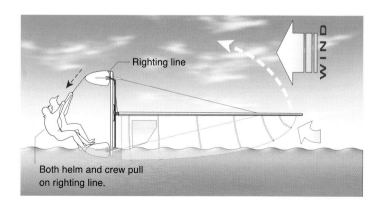

Righting line

Both helm and crew pull on righting line.

ORIENTATING THE BOAT

Righting lines

A number of dinghies now have righting lines, usually stowed under the gunwale and retained by elastic. These can be helpful in balancing on the centreboard or while leaning back to right the boat.

Both dinghies and multihulls can be spun around as desired by lifting the mast clear of the water and driving it around.

If there is a spinnaker up, drop it before righting the boat.

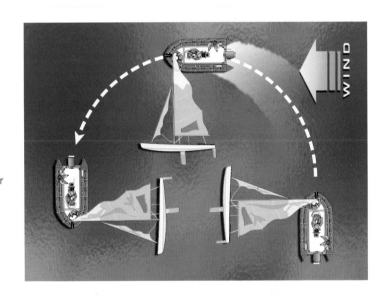

After righting

In general once a boat is upright and the crew out of the water, hold the safety boat firmly alongside the windward side of any boat and use the safety boat engine to manoeuvre both as necessary. Beware of lines fouling the propeller.

Safety Boat Handbook

Safety Guidelines

- Take care not to injure anyone, including yourself.
- Approach slowly, if possible using the wind to stop the boat, not the engine.
- Switch off the engine as soon as there is contact with the person.
- Help them aboard over the lowest part of the side of the boat.
- If the person in the water is conscious, they can often help themselves into the safety boat,with assistance from the crew.

- Take care lifting people, keep low in the boat to avoid straining your back.
- If a casualty is unconscious, call for help by radio or other means as soon as possible.
- Before restarting the engine and driving away, make sure that any passengers are properly seated and holding on. Unconscious casualties should be on the floor area of the boat, with their head supported.

THE BASIC LIFT

Turn the engine off. Move the person to the lowest part of the boat, facing in towards the safety boat. Provided there are no other considerations the helm can leave the driving seat and lend a hand.

The person in the water will naturally reach up to hold onto the gunwale. Reach down, get a firm grip on clothing around the legs or waist area.

If possible working with another, carefully ease the person over the gunwale and onto the floor of the boat.

In heavy conditions, the person's legs may trail under the hull of the boat, making it difficult to haul them in. Turn them around so that they face away from the boat, and then haul them on to the side. N.B. This method is strenuous and can disorientate the casualty.

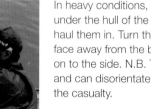

THE ROLL/SLIDE

Lie the conscious person alongside the lowest part of the boat, with their head towards the bow. Lift one leg up onto the side with their hands on the side of the boat. Reach down to get a firm grip of the person or their clothing, and part slide/part roll them aboard.

USING THE ENGINE AS A STEP

> **Caution**
>
> This is only sensible in calm water or injury may result

Make sure that the engine is switched off, and that their clothing does not foul on the engine or other protrusions. Ask the person in the water to use the anti-ventilation plate on the engine as a foot step. Advise them where to take a handhold, avoiding any grease or other lubricants on the engine. Beware in waves, where the movement of the boat may injure the person on the engine.

RIBS ONLY – DEFLATE A SPONSON

If the person in the water is too heavy to lift, or cannot help themselves out using the engine as a foothold, part of the inflatable sponson can be deflated. Bring the person alongside, make sure they have a firm hold on the boat and then partially deflate the tube by opening the air valve. Once aboard, the tube can be re-inflated using the boat's foot pump. This method can also be used to bring unconscious casualties aboard.

In an emergency, most RIBs can be driven with partially deflated tubes.

USING A JASON'S CRADLE

A Jason's Cradle is a roll of mesh or a roll-up framework fixed to the side of the safety boat. The cradle can be unrolled and the person floated into the cradle, before rolling them into the safety boat.

> **Caution**
>
> Whilst cradles make lifting significantly easier the rolling action can sometimes disorientate the casualty, or induce dizziness.

On a safety boat two pairs of hands are better than one, particularly if the workload is likely to be high, but the decision will depend on a number of factors. It may be perfectly in order to drive solo in a safety boat, particularly in conjunction with colleagues in other boats.

A small group of single-handed dinghies can usually be supported or instructed by a solo instructor, but dealing with a bigger capsized dinghy is easier with two people. Other jobs such as lifting and moving racing buoys are much easier with two.

Remember that the crew of the boat you are assisting may well be able to do most of the work!

Serious incidents and even fatalities have occurred because the safety crews were unable to recover heavy sailors from the water, so consider all relevant factors in crewing up the safety cover. Can you provide effective cover for everyone afloat?

CLOTHING AND PERSONAL EQUIPMENT

The safety boat crew should be willing to enter the water in carrying out their duties. It is important to be prepared – here are some things to think about:

In general a buoyancy aid is more suitable than a lifejacket because it allows considerable mobility in the water.

Buoyancy aid

An inflated lifejacket is cumbersome, allows little movement in the water and often snags on rigging etc. However in certain conditions, such as coaching in hot weather, there may be arguments for a manual gas inflation lifejacket.

Lifejacket

Safety boat crews often sit still in the boat for a long time, so it pays to stay dry. A drysuit is a wonderful asset if you have one. A wetsuit and waterproofs can also be very effective.

Exposure to sun can be a problem, so appropriate clothing, sun cream, sunglasses, a drink and sun hat are a good idea. It goes without saying that it is good practice for everyone afloat to carry a knife. There should always be a sharp, serrated knife instantly available in the safety boat.

See page 52 for full details of safety equipment for the boat.

Your strategy will depend on your role. A group of novice sailors will normally receive close attention from a qualified instructor, providing both tuition and safety cover. The safety boat is therefore fundamental to their safety. There might be other safety boats providing extra support.

On the other hand a fleet of racing dinghies will require safety boats which will not normally intervene at each capsize, but only if required. Outside intervention disqualifies the sailors from the race, so you will usually only become directly involved if the sailors are tired, conditions have become extreme, or something has broken. Sailors will frequently be grateful for a tow home if the wind has dropped after the race!

COMMUNICATION

Safety during tuition or racing will depend on good communication as much as anything else. A small group of Oppies on a sheltered lake will require a different communication network to a national coastal regatta. Simple is usually best: remember that radios can be very useful but do go overboard and batteries do run down. Simple signals are useful if everyone understands them.

Communication: Golden Rules

- If using hand signals ensure everyone understands them; keep signals few and simple.

- When you want to talk to someone, get in close and preferably upwind. If possible, turn the engine off. Ideally both parties should be able to talk without raising their voices.

- If information is being passed or signals being used, ensure that the receiving party acknowledges that they have indeed understood.

If communicating over greater distances, the most common solution is to use marine VHF radio equipment. The choices range from hand-held waterproof sets to fixed, built in ones offering a number of working channels with a DSC distress facility. Some sets can have a private channel so that operating conversations don't block the other airwaves used by the general public.

Reliability is important, so do all you can to protect the radio. Do not locate fixed sets where they will be vulnerable to damage.

Training in how to use VHF equipment properly is available at RYA training centres around the country. See the RYA website for details.

Hand signals can be effective over quite long distances

It is useful to have a trained first aider on site when sailing is taking place. The RYA first aid course covers the basics, and the knowledge gained can make a difference in an emergency.

Golden Rule

- The guiding principle in the event of an injury afloat is that the safety boat crew should "scoop and run" the casualty back to the shore.

In some situations, such as when at sea some way from the shore, it may be worth having a trained person on each safety boat who can give first aid whilst in transit.

Cold and hypothermia are a regular problem in the UK, and the wind chill effect on a cold, wet casualty at speed in the safety boat can be serious. Beware of complicated systems for wrapping people up: simple is best. A bin liner with holes for arms and head, or a survival bag can be very effective.

RYA first aid courses are available at many sailing clubs and sailing centres. A list of courses can be accessed from the RYA website.

The exact contents of a safety boat first aid kit will vary according to the location and the degree of isolation. All first aid kits should be in a waterproof container and should be checked regularly. It is often better to store the kit outside the boat with the lid off when the boat is ashore: Kits stored in boats usually get damp. See the Guidance Notes for the Inspection of RYA Recognised Training Centres for a list of the minimum first aid kit contents for training centres.

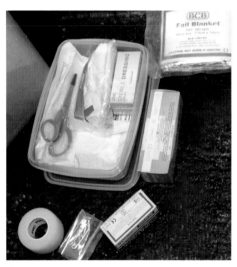

These boats are generally sailed in small fleets to introduce novices to sailing. They are likely to have small, unstayed rigs and plastic hulls. The rescue methods are designed to get the novice sailor up and sailing again as soon as possible.

 DINGHY CAPSIZED, CREW BY DAGGERBOARD

Position the safety boat at the tip of the mast, preferably facing the same direction as the dinghy, with the engine off. Lift the tip of the mast to begin righting. (Often this is all that is required).

Work slowly down the mast, until the dinghy is upright and the safety boat is almost alongside the dinghy. Once the crew has climbed aboard, ensure they are able to continue.

If the crew is separated from their boat, it's possible to recover them in the usual manner, before positioning the safety boat alongside the dinghy hull, facing in the same direction if possible.

Apply downward pressure on the daggerboard to right the boat, ensuring that it does not foul the gunwale of the safety boat.

Take care that as the dinghy rights, the boom doesn't swing over the safety boat and strike any of its occupants. The best solution is usually to rotate the boat so the rig is lying downwind of the hull, causing the boom to blow away from the safety boat once the dinghy is upright.

Return the crew to the craft so they can continue sailing.

SHORT TOW

Novices often drift downwind out of the sailing area, requiring a tow upwind. Bring the sailor into the safety boat. Position the safety boat at the mast tip, facing the same way as the dinghy. Keeping the mast low, draw the rig across the safety boat until the boom reaches the gunwale of the safety boat. If the safety boat has console steering, the helm can sit on the mast, with the dinghy crew also holding onto it. If the safety boat has tiller steering, then the dinghy crew will have to hold the mast on their own. The dinghy can then be motored slowly back to the sailing area. Take care when moving off lest lines foul the prop. Once under way any lines will stream aft, clear of the prop. Once in the sailing area, position the safety boat upwind of the dinghy, so that when the mast is lifted to right it, the boom can swing freely away from the safety boat occupants with the sail flapping.

Optimist dinghies and their 'plastic' equivalents are ideal craft for teaching very young novice sailors. However, when they capsize, the enclosed gunwales make it almost impossible for the novice to recover unaided. If they do come upright, the boat will be waterlogged so it will be necessary for the safety boat crew to help. They often invert – see 'Inverted Dinghies' for solutions.

CRAFT CAPSIZED AND WATERLOGGED

1. Bring the crew into the safety boat using the usual MOB method.

2. Position the safety boat by the dinghy bow and at 90° to the dinghy, with the mast lying along the surface of the water.

3. Draw the craft up and over the gunwale, onto the safety boat. The dinghy will drain during this manoeuvre.

4. Once the dinghy is on the safety boat, remove the daggerboard. Now the dinghy can be righted whilst still on board the safety boat.

5. Slide the dinghy back into the water. Replace the daggerboard. Replace the crew. The dinghy crew can then resume sailing.

SHORT TOWS

If the dinghy has drifted downwind of the sailing area, it can be left on the safety boat whilst it is motored gently back to the course, thereby saving the necessity of using a towline.

If this distance is large, the rig can be removed completely and stowed temporarily in the safety boat.

The hull can remain on the safety boat.

On the rare occasions that experienced crews need help, it is likely to be due to fatigue or gear failure. Less experienced crews can suffer multiple capsizes, particularly if the breeze increases, and may become exhausted and need recovering to the shore.

Experienced sailors may know how best to deal with a problem themselves, but remember that you are responsible for the safety boat itself. Often only a steadying hand on the tip of the rig is required whilst the crew sort out the problem.

The principles for high performance boats are the same as for most other double-handed sailing craft, but the boats are fragile, light and powerful.

If the boat capsized with the spinnaker up, it must be dropped and stowed before righting. This can usually be done by the crew, often by pulling a single line.

Some boats have righting lines stowed under the gunwale. These are used to keep the crew stable on the centreboard as they pull the boat up.

Always stay alongside until the crew have everything under control.

DINGHY CAPSIZED, CREW ABLE TO ASSIST

Approach the dinghy at the forestay and hold the mast or forestay to prevent the boat from inverting.

Ask the crew to drop the spinnaker, ease kicker and free sheets.

Gently motor the mast around downwind of the dinghy hull. The righting action will then be towards the wind and controlled.

Check that the helm is ready on the centreboard and the crew is in the water between the hull and boom, ready to be 'scooped' up by the hull.

Golden Rule

- Before righting de-power the rig by releasing tension off the kicking strap, and uncleating jib and mainsheets. This will ease handling once upright.

Slowly raise the mast up to start the dinghy righting.

The dinghy crew now continues righting, pulling the rig up and into the wind.

For a high performance boat or if the crew are light or tired, the safety boat motors the mast round so that it points upwind and the breeze assists with the righting. Confirm with the crew that they are ready as the boat may come up quickly.

Classes which are not self-draining may need support alongside whilst baling out.

TOW THE BOAT UP

Attach a line onto the painter of the safety boat. Position the safety boat upwind and bow-in to the dinghy, forward of the centreboard. Pass the line to whoever is on the centreboard.

Tie or clip the line onto the top jib sheet. For a high performance boat attach the line onto the shroud where it joins the hull, or the rack (if it has one).

The dinghy crew should stay on the centreboard, as the safety boat reverses away paying out the remaining tow-line, at 90° to the dinghy.

Once the strain is on the tow-line, the cox'n gently increases power in reverse to start bringing the dinghy upright.

As the dinghy rights, the dinghy helmsman can step over the gunwale, therefore balancing the dinghy. This may at times be difficult: it is also possible to board over the side or stern.

Once the dinghy is righted, the safety boat makes its way back down the tow-line keeping pressure on it to prevent the dinghy re-capsizing, it then recovers the tow-line.

The safety boat stays upwind and alongside the dinghy until the dinghy crew are ready.

Safety Boat Handbook

On windy days fast cats are quicker than most safety boats. Because of their wide beam and powerful rig the issues for safety boats are slightly different to monohull dinghies.

Many cats have sealed, buoyant masts which reduce the tendency to invert. Despite this it is usually worth holding the mast tip to keep it on the surface. Most cats will have a 'righting line' attached to the base of the mast, usually stowed in a bag on the trampoline. Find this (or improvise one) and de-power the rig before righting, or the boat may be uncontrollable once upright.

 THE 'MAST FLIP'

1. Position the safety boat at the tip of the mast. Check that the main sheet is un-cleated and the traveller is released.

4. Eventually, the crew will be able to take over and right the cat.

2. With the safety boat crew holding the tip of the mast, motor the mast slowly around and into the wind.

5. The cat crew must be careful that as it rights, they are not struck by the top hull coming down, they should also be ready to hold down the cross beam to prevent the cat capsizing again. Once the cat is upright, come alongside the windward hull and control the cat using the safety boat engine.

3. Having checked the crew is ready, slowly raise the mast tip up. Gently work down the mast towards the hulls, raising it at the same time.

Golden Rule

De-power the mainsail before righting a multi-hull. Do this by un-cleating the mainsheet and the traveller (a track for the mainsheet across the back of the boat)

TOW THE BOAT UP

1. Prepare a towline with clip, attached to the safety boat painter. Position the safety boat at 90°, bow in to the cat's lower hull. Check that the mainsheet and traveller are released.

2. Attach the towline to the cat's righting line, having first checked that it has passed from the base of the mast, up and over the top hull and back down over the reverse side of the trampoline to the crew. Gently reverse away from the cat to take up the slack in the towline. Begin the righting process by gently increasing throttle and keeping the tensioned towline at 90°.

3. Before the cat rights, check that the crew are ready.

4. Once the cat is righted, the safety boat crew makes its way back down the towline to recover it and check the crew are able to continue.

Safety Boat Handbook

SINGLE-HANDED DINGHY

DOUBLE-HANDED DINGHY

Position the safety boat alongside the upturned hull, if possible facing in the same direction. Bring the crew into the safety boat and apply pressure on the daggerboard pulling it towards the safety boat.

Ask the crew to find and hold a jib sheet (if possible the down-wind one). Safety boat crew prepares a towline, as above. Safety boat approaches the middle of the dinghy bow-in and upwind. The towline is attached over the hull, behind the daggerboard and onto the further jib sheet.

Placing a foot on the dinghy's gunwale may help break the suction effect of the upturned hull.

Once the hull is at 90°, continue as normal.

Sometimes the daggerboard may drop down through the hull, leaving nothing to right the dinghy with. If free it can often be re-inserted directly into the case from above. Ensure it goes right through the full height of the case before levering, or the case may be damaged by the end of the board as you lever it.

The safety boat reverses away upwind and takes the strain on the towline. Keeping the towline at 90° to the dinghy, the safety boat continues reversing, applying tension to the line.

Top Tip
If the board is missing use a paddle inserted into the dagger board slot, do not apply too much pressure as the paddle may snap.

This will start righting the dinghy.

N.B. As the dinghy passes through 90° with its mast parallel to the water, the crew may climb over the gunwale to balance the righted boat, though this is often difficult to do.

Once the rig reaches the surface there are several options, but the simplest is often to continue reversing bringing the boat upright.

Once the dinghy is righted, the towline is recovered by motoring gently back to the hull, keeping a little tension on the line to stabilise the boat.

Top tip

The centreboard sometimes drops into the case completely. Going under the boat to lower (raise) the centreboard can be uncomfortable. Centreboards on training dinghies can often be 'fished' out of the case with a loop of string such as your knife lanyard.

HIGH PERFORMANCE BOATS
There are four principle methods.

Method 1 Extra leverage on centre board

With the safety boat alongside the inverted dinghy, get both helm and crew to stand on the near gunwale, holding onto the centreboard. Dinghy crew and safety boat crew lean back on the centreboard as normal. Be careful not to snap the board. Once the dinghy starts to right, its crew should be able to continue without assistance. Safety boat stands off to check all is well.

Method 2 Tow the boat up

This is similar to the technique described in Method 1 for two-person dinghies. Position the safety boat bow-in towards the daggerboard, preferably on the upwind side of the dinghy hull. (Continued on page 26)

Safety Boat Handbook

(Continued from page 25) Attach a line from the safety boat (attached to the safety boat painter) over the hull, behind the daggerboard and onto the downwind rack or to the shroud where it joins the hull. Gently motor astern and upwind, taking up the slack, then applying pressure while maintaining the safety boat at right angles to the dinghy. Continue reversing until the mast is lying on the surface of the water. If the spinnaker was hoisted, the crew can now drop it. The helm remains on the centreboard to assist with the righting.

Once the spinnaker is stowed and the kicker and sheets released, the safety boat can continue to apply pressure on the towline until the dinghy is righted.

The safety boat crew can then recover the towline hand over hand, keeping light pressure on it to stop the dinghy from capsizing again.

Remain alongside while the crew sort themselves out.

 ## Method 3 Spinning with Power

This method may possibly cause damage to the spinnaker (with the prop) or pole. It is ineffective if the mast is touching the bottom.

Recover crew then use the power of the safety boat to rotate the dinghy.

Position the safety boat at the bow of the inverted dinghy and at 90° to it.

The safety boat crew passes their painter around the pole or forestay, and holds it tightly or makes it fast in their boat.

The safety boat cox'n then powers forward, keeping the safety boat at 90° to the dinghy.

This will cause the dinghy to right towards the safety boat.

Once the forestay becomes visible, power is taken off and the safety boat crew take hold of it to prevent the dinghy re-capsizing.

Caution

Methods 3 and 4 should be regarded only as a last resort.

Top tip

Once the rig is on the surface get the spinnaker down and release sheets and kicker.

Method 4 Use the spinnaker

Another last resort for asymmetric dinghies with the spinnaker raised is to drag the rig to the surface using the spinnaker and halyard.

Detach or cut the spinnaker tack line (the line that joins the bottom corner of the spinnaker to the end of the pole) and hold the corner of the spinnaker from the safety boat bow.

Back the safety boat away a short distance, at 90° to the upturned hull. The safety boat crew then starts to gather up the spinnaker, drawing the mast to the surface.

Once the mast is at the surface, the dinghy can be stabilised by the safety boat.

If the spinnaker is not raised, locate the halyard as it exits the spinnaker chute, cut and hold it from the safety boat bow, and follow the above procedure.

Safety Boat Handbook

CAT INVERTED, CREW IN NEED OF ASSISTANCE

Prepare the towline and check that the mainsheet and traveller have been released.

1. Position the safety boat at 90° to the upwind hull, bow in. Attach the towline to the righting line having checked that it has been led correctly from the base of the mast, up around and over the downwind hull and back over the upturned trampoline. Gently reverse away from the cat to take up the slack in the towline.

2. Apply tension to the towline by continuing to reverse with power. The cat crew can assist by positioning themselves at the stern of the windward hull.

3. Because of resistance to the water from its rig, the cat will come up to the 90° capsized position as described above.

Top tip

Capsized multihulls tend to pivot in the breeze – the hull blows downwind of the rig, and the wind under the rig helps to right the boat. If the wind flips the boat over as soon as it comes upright, the rig may hit the safety boat, so use a long towline to keep clear.

4. The safety boat continues reversing and as the cat nears righting, check that the crew are ready to take hold of the dolphin striker/front cross beam to prevent the cat re-capsizing.

Once the craft is righted, the safety boat crew can make its way back down the towline to recover it and check with the crew.

5. Towing boats upright is an uncertain business and even experienced crews get it wrong sometimes!

DINGHIES

Boats in this position will usually require help from the safety boat. Be very careful not to damage the rig by putting weight on the upturned hull, or pulling too hard or in the wrong direction.

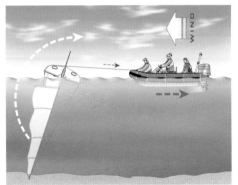

1. The technique is much the same as for a double-handed inversion (see page 24), however it is important the rig is pulled out from the same direction as it went in. If the dinghy is not fully inverted one gunwale will be higher than the other.

   Position the safety boat alongside the lower gunwale of the upturned hull.

2. Take the jib sheet from the higher side, over the hull and behind the centre board, clipping a towline to it from the safety boat. Fasten the towline to the safety boat painter.

3. In the case of a single-handed dinghy, pass the towline with a clip over the gunhale, around the mast and back onto itself.

4. Re-start the engine and reverse gently away from the dinghy keeping the line at 90° to the hull. Once the slack has been taken out carefully apply more power to draw the mast out of the mud.

5. Keep reversing until the dinghy is fully upright. Alternatively once the rig reaches the surface, cease reversing and gather in the tensioned line, drawing the dinghy to the safety boat. Once alongside, recover the dinghy as normal.

MULTIHULLS

It should be possible to tell when the mast is in the mud because one hull will be higher than the other or out of the water completely. The risk of rig damage is the same as for dinghies, so be careful.

Approach the lower hull with the towline prepared as for other rescues. Follow the sequence for an inverted cat (see page 28), applying tension carefully to the towline as the mast releases from the mud.

Notes

When using a towline to right a boat in reasonably calm water, the safety boat can be reversed away from the rescue with its propeller away from anything vulnerable.

In exposed conditions or waves this method will cause the safety boat to take on water, so it may be necessary to carry out rescues with the safety boat's bow into the waves. Care is required because this will decrease the cox'n's view of the operation and put the propeller closer to the towline and the rescue.

Dinghy sailing is a very safe sport, but on rare occasions sailors have been tangled under an inverting boat. Many modern boats are self-draining resulting in there being little or no air gap underneath when the craft inverts. In waves, there will be virtually no air gap under any dinghy. Incidents of this type can be alarming or worse so safety boat crews should be alert to this possibility.

PREVENTING INVERSIONS

If appropriate during dinghy training sessions, boats can be prevented from inverting by tying an air bag to the top of the mainsail.

A 30L float on a short lanyard prevents most inversions, and lets some water on the sail to prevent the boat flipping up before the crew are ready.

Most dinghies will invert following a windward capsize, in wind over tide, or if simply left for a while on their side. During training the safety boat can provide a useful service in preventing inversions by holding the mast tip or supporting the forestay.

DINGHY INVERTED, SUSPECTED MISSING CREW MEMBER

If one of the crew is known to be trapped under the dinghy, call for help as soon as possible via VHF with a Mayday call, or via the base station ashore.

1. The best strategy is usually to right the boat. Ask the remaining sailor for information on the missing crew member's last location.

2. Drive the safety boat immediately to the centreboard. One of the safety boat crew then boards the inverted hull by the centreboard. Caution, this will reduce the air gap under the hull.

Warning

Always beware of the prop – engine off or neutral whenever possible.

3. Using the combined weight of the safety boat crew and the remaining sailor, apply sideways pressure to the centreboard to initiate righting.

4. Take the safety boat to the bow of the dinghy where the driver can hold the emerging forestay to assist with righting. As the rig reaches the surface, the safety boat can stabilise the dinghy using the forestay.

5. The safety boat crew can now see into the dinghy and the missing person should be on the surface.

SOLO DRIVER IN SAFETY BOAT

- You may be alone driving the safety boat, or rescuing a single-hander. These situations require slightly different approaches, and a problem-solving approach is required:

- If possible, get the crew to help by pulling on the centreboard.

- Start righting the boat by levering on the centreboard, transferring to the forestay as the rig reaches the surface.

- As a last resort the driver may transfer their full weight to the centreboard, retaining a hold on the painter of the safety boat.

A driver who has fallen into the water during this type of rescue should be able to re-board using the anti-ventilation plates as a step, though this can be very difficult in heavy wet gear.

SINGLE HANDERS

Picos, Lasers and even trapeze single-handers are relatively light, safety boat crews may therefore be able to lift the bow onto the gunwale/sponson of the safety boat, creating an air gap underneath.

Safety Boat Handbook

Getting a crew and/or boat off a lee shore can be challenging. Care and planning are required or the safety boat may join the first boat on the shore! The usual scenario will be that a dinghy has ended up on a lee shore and is unable to make its way back out to deeper water. The first priority is to make sure that the safety boat is positioned in a safe area.

1. Anchor in this safe position, then make certain that the anchor is holding by using transits.

2. This is one of the few occasions where the engine can be left running.

3. A line can then be transferred ashore. Attach a float (fender) to the end of the line and allow it to drift in. Several lines may need to be tied together in order to achieve this. If the safety boat is close enough, a heaving line can be thrown instead.

4. Once the dinghy crew have recovered the line and attached it to their craft, the safety boat crew can haul the dinghy out from the shore to the safety boat itself. The dinghy can then be towed in the usual manner, or the crew can continue to sail.

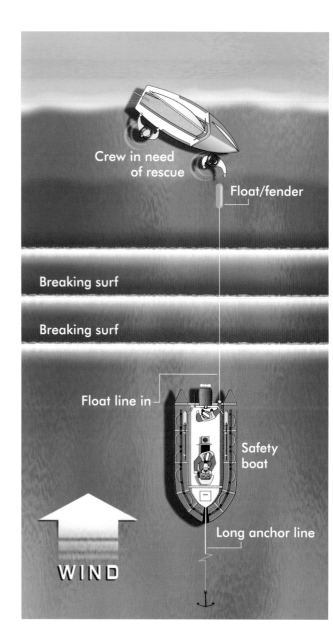

Crew in need of rescue

Float/fender

Breaking surf

Breaking surf

Float line in

Safety boat

Long anchor line

WIND

BREAKING SURF

Breaking surf can be a real problem.

In general do not drive in through surf, anchor the safety boat outside the surf break (check the anchor is holding) and then float a line in.
Once the line is ashore and attached, the dinghy can be hauled out through the surf.

Caution

This method is not without risk to both parties, so the safety boat crew should consider all possible outcomes before attempting to rescue a craft which is, in effect, safely ashore.

CONCRETE DAMS

Concrete dam walls can be particularly difficult because they are slippery and it is difficult to anchor close by in the deep water. In this situation you may have to lengthen the anchor warp. At this type of venue it is worth carrying a suitable warp. Alternatively, it may be possible to point the safety boat into the wind, hold off the dam using the engine and throw a heaving line.

Windsurfers are generally prepared for immersion, so they are likely to be wearing a wetsuit (in UK waters). If they have been in the water for a while they may not necessarily be in difficulty, however, when approaching a windsurfer, the fundamental principle of 'people first, kit second' still applies.

 SIMPLE RECOVERY

This is common in a teaching environment, where the novice windsurfer has drifted downwind or down tide. You will usually find small rigs and large boards which support the windsurfer's weight at rest.

- Approach the windsurfer and equipment from the mast tip (Usually the most upwind part). Ask them to sit on their board and make contact with the mast tip, with the safety boat facing the same way as the board.

- Switch off the engine.

- The safety boat crew then makes their way down the mast along the luff (mast edge) of the sail, drawing the rig over the safety boat and the board and sailor closer.

- When the board is next to the boat, the windsurfer can step into the safety boat.

- If possible bring the boom into the boat to help keep the board alongside.

- If there is a daggerboard, raise it.

- Lie the rig across the boat with the mast foremost (and into the wind). On a tiller steered safety boat, the windsurfer can face aft and hold the mast/rig down. On a central console boat, it may be easier for the driver to sit on the mast whilst the windsurfer sits on the side away from the board, helping to hold the mast down.

- The engine can then be re-started, and boat and board driven off together.

Usually the windsurfer will need to go upwind. If the sailor has to be taken downwind, reverse the rig so that the mast is still facing towards the wind.

 HIGH WIND

Windsurfers in high winds will probably be using a big powerful rig made of fragile material and a short board which may not support the weight of the windsurfer at rest.
Take care lifting the rig above the level of the water – it will have huge power and the wind may cause it to 'fly'.

Usually the 'simple recovery' is effective, but there are two alternatives depending on conditions:

Alternative 1: Detach the Rig from the Board

Make contact with the tip of the mast. Switch off the engine.

Work carefully down the mast until the windsurfer and board are reached.

Bring the windsurfer into the safety boat to assist with rescue.

Detach the board from the rig, usually a button/pin system. Stow the board in the safety boat.

Secure the rig across the safety boat, ensuring that the luff will face into wind.

Motor slowly to safety.

Alternative 2: De-rig the Sail

You may choose to stow the board as in method 1 and de-rig the sail. Ask the windsurfer to do this, if possible. If not:

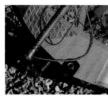

Release the outhaul, (jam cleat at the end of the boom).

Remove the boom, (lever cam on mast end of boom) and stow it in the safety boat.

Release the downhaul, (multi purchase jam cleat at bottom of mast. Take care as there is a huge load on the purchase system).

Undo the downhaul line from the pulleys. and remove the mast extension.

Remove the mast from the sail by gathering it up towards the mast tip.

Stow the mast, which will be in 2 sections.

Roll (don't fold) the sail from its head to its foot into a tube shape. Stow the sail.

Return all to safety.

Safety Boat Handbook

Groups of canoeists and kayakers (paddlers) are generally self-sufficient afloat. On occasion you may encounter a paddler in need of assistance by a safety boat and novice sea kayaking groups are sometimes escorted by power boats.

Kayaks are 'sit on' or 'sit in' craft with double-bladed paddles. Canoes are open boats with single bladed paddles.

As usual recover the person first. Capsized boats are easily damaged (and the risk of injury increased) if you try to lift them when full of water, so the trick is to drain them first.

KAYAKER REQUIRING ASSISTANCE

Attempting to drive alongside a kayak may well capsize it. It is safer to drive near to the paddler and allow them to come to you. The paddler may prefer to use their paddle as a 'bridge' between the safety boat and their kayak, or to pass you the paddle first. At this point the paddler is most vulnerable.

The paddler removes their spraydeck and shuffles back onto the rear deck of the kayak.

Whilst staying low, the paddler slides across towards the safety boat placing the nearest leg into the safety boat. They then slide onto the gunwale of the safety boat before sliding the remaining leg across.

The kayak can be stowed either along the safety boat or across it and all can be returned to safety.

 CAPSIZED KAYAKER WHO HAS FALLEN OUT OF THEIR BOAT

Recover the paddler with the normal MOB method (see page 8), if possible without losing the kayak.

Having made contact with the kayak, (if it is inverted, then leave it like that) position the kayak's bow towards the safety boat, and at 90°.

Lift the bow onto the gunwale of the safety boat. It will partially drain, especially if fitted with air bags in the stern section.

Slide the kayak over the safety boat until it naturally over-balances itself.

Do not push down on the kayak to assist this process. The kayak will empty into the safety boat, which can be drained later. Stow the kayak as described on previous page.

Sea kayaks are much longer than general purpose kayaks and can be emptied in the same way. However they are fragile and should be handled carefully to avoid damage. A waterlogged kayak too heavy to lift as above, or a flooded sea kayak, should be handled as follows:

THE 'CURL' METHOD

Position the waterlogged kayak on its side and parallel to the safety boat with the cockpit towards you.

The rescuer should then place their elbows on the gunwale of the safety boat, with upturned hands under the upper rim of the cockpit.

Apply and maintain steady upward pressure to the rim. This slightly raises the water level inside the kayak, causing it to drain.

When the kayak feels light enough, swing it through 90° across the safety boat and continue to empty it as described above.

OPEN CANOES

Open canoes are vulnerable in strong winds and very heavy when swamped. However, they are easy to recover.

1. Recover the crew with the usual MOB (see page 8) method.

2. Get the canoe at 90° to the safety boat.

4. Allow the canoe to overbalance onto the safety boat itself. At this point, the canoe should be empty.

3. With the canoe on its side, draw it across the safety boat, keeping the 90° alignment.

5. Either stow the canoe on the safety boat and return all to the shore, or having righted the canoe whilst still on the safety boat, slide it back into the water and assist the crew back into it.

Many outdoor centres offer a wide range of activities which require support and safety cover from power boats. These range from rafted canoe trips in sheltered coastal water to problem solving activities using barrels and logs, or orienteering afloat.

Each centre should provide specific training for these activities, but the general principles outlined in this book still apply to providers of safety cover.

Golden Rules

- Wear the kill cord at all times when the engine is on.

- Count heads.

- Recover people before kit.

- Always turn the engine off when in contact with people in the water.

Rafted canoes should be lashed with their bows slightly closer together than their sterns. Failure to do this can result in a standing wave building between the hulls, swamping the raft. Rafted canoes are best towed empty to prevent this – putting at least some of the crew in the tug lightens the tow and reduces wave-making.

RAFTED CANOES

These provide a very stable platform for a group to paddle but are difficult to deal with if swamped. The best approach is often to beach the raft and disassemble, or if necessary to disassemble afloat before emptying the canoes in the normal way.

RAFT BUILDING

A capsizing or disintegrating raft usually results in the entire crew being dumped into the water. You will therefore be operating with the engine off, and there is an argument for utilising a rowing boat, which can manoeuvre safely in this situation, rather than a power boat. Rafts are vulnerable to wind and tide. They can be towed astern on a long tow.

Safety Boat Handbook

Kite surfing is a new and developing sport. Kitesurfers are propelled on their boards by a powerful canopy with different sizes of kite used depending on the wind strength. Safety boat drivers may encounter kitesurfers in need of assistance; the kitesurfer is likely to be the best source of information about their own equipment.

Two main types of kite are in use:

a. The foil kite, usually in smaller sizes, generally have 'value systems' built into the leading edge to keep them inflated if they crash onto the water.

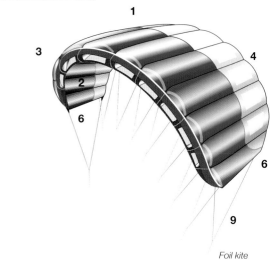

Foil kite

b. The more common leading edge inflatable kites (LEI), have supporting inflatable ribs to give the kite its shape. The LEI will have an inflation/deflation valve and sometimes an emergency dump valve located in the centre of the leading edge bladder, which when opened will collapse the leading edge, de-powering the kite.

Kite Parts

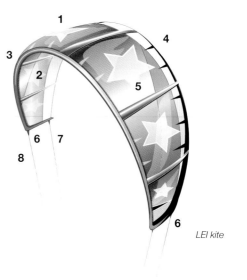

LEI kite

1	top skin
2	lower skin
3	leading edge
4	trailing edge
5	struts
6	wingtips
7	back pig tail or connecting knot
8	front pig tail or connecting knot
9	bridles

Kite boards are short and provide little buoyancy for the kitesurfer when at rest. If the kite cannot be re-launched in light winds the kitesurfer has limited options. In windy conditions, an overpowered kite can become a hazard to the rider and other water users.

APPROACHING A DOWNED KITESURFER

• Approach the rider on a line from them that is approx. 90° to the wind, keeping to the sector shown as green in the illustrations. This will keep the safety boat clear of any trailing broken lines or the kite board which may be upwind of the rider – (see the yellow sector in diagrams). The main kite lines and kite will be downwind of the kitesurfer.

• Make contact with the rider so that they are on the downwind side of the safety boat. Check that the rider is OK before deciding on your strategy – follow the recovery rules below.

Four recovery methods

Method 1 Rider packs kite away
If the kitesurfer is not in danger from the elements ask them to pack away their kite and its lines (see Diagram 1).

Stand by to pick them up once they have done this. Never try to re-launch the kite for them unless you have been trained to do so.

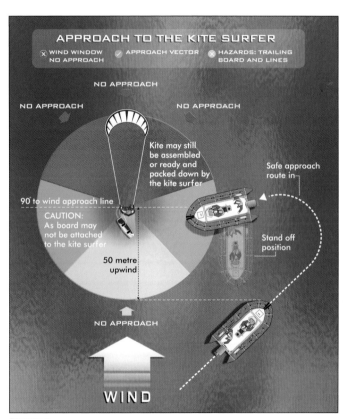

Diagram 1

Golden Rule

Do not begin the rescue from where the rider is by drawing the kite in towards the boat. Accidents have occurred when the kite has re-launched itself whilst the rescuer has been working down the lines towards the kite. The control lines turn rapidly into very effective blades, which can slice fingers to the bone.

Method 2 Kite requires pack up
If the rider is unable to coil in and pack down, but is uninjured, ask them to 'leash out or de-power the kite'.

- Drive the safety boat to the kite, keeping clear of the red zone (see diagram 2).

- Approach from downwind, with the crew member keeping low in the bow of the boat ready to make contact with the kite. **Take care at all times that the kite does not re-launch itself**.

- Once in contact keep the kite low to the water and deflate using the valve, generally found in the middle of the leading edge. Do not try to turn the kite over in the water and on no account hold or grab the strings/lines whilst doing this.

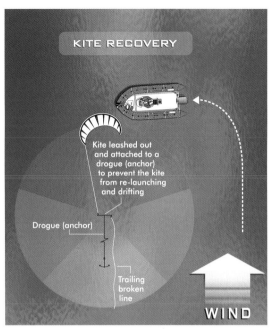

KITE RECOVERY

Kite leashed out and attached to a drogue (anchor) to prevent the kite from re-launching and drifting

Drogue (anchor)

Trailing broken line

WIND

Diagram 2

- Disconnect the control lines from the pigtails. The connection is a larks foot knot, which is easily undone when the tension is removed from the lines either side of the knot.

- Once the bladder is deflated, the kite will be de-powered and is unlikely to re-launch.

- Gather the kite into the safety boat, pulling the canopy between your legs, sitting on it as you do so.

- Knot all four lines together and place them in the water. Then signal the rider to coil the lines up on their bar. It is important not to release the lines one at a time or they become tangled.

- Roll the kite along its remaining inflated ribs from one end to the middle, and then repeat the process from the other end. Stow kite and board in the safety boat.

- Once the rider has retrieved all their lines pick them up in the normal way and return them and their kit to safety.

Method 3 Injured rider

If the rider is badly injured then you must make a decision on whether to release the kite completely or even to cut the rider free of the kite.

Once unhooked from the control bar the rider will still be attached to the safety leash.

- An abandoned kite is a hazard, so if possible replace the rider's weight on the safety leash with a drogue or improvised sea anchor. This can be a difficult decision because an ineffective drogue can also pose a real threat. The anchor is an obvious choice, but could increase the risk if it failed to hold.

- As always if the rider is able, get them to 'leash the kite out' i.e. activate the safety system to de-power the kite, and take their advice on how to abandon the kite safely.

- If you are using a drogue then attach this to the end of the rider's leash and attach a float to the bar. This will help later in recovery of the kite, by making it easy to locate the bar.

- Recover the rider, administer first aid and evacuate to the shore.

- The kite should not drift far if the drogue is effective.

- If you return later to collect the kite, follow the procedure as in recovery method 2. However once you have the kite and have disconnected the lines, return to the bar, retrieve it and coil in the lines. If you have not used a float this will not be possible and you will have to pull the lines slowly onto the boat, stowing them into a bucket or inside the kite canopy.

Method 4 Recovering a drogued kite

- First get downwind of the kite, taking care not to run over the lines or bar as you chase it.

- Approach the kite and recovery cautiously as in the recovery methods 2 and 3.

- Once the kite is aboard pull in the bar and lines, either stowing into a bucket or the kite canopy.

Safety boat crews at clubs or events may be asked to lay the racing marks indicating the course to be used. This is easy on inland water because the water level does not change. If the location is tidal and the mark to be in place for some hours, a little more preparation may be required.

INLAND LOCATION

Laying the mark

Marker buoys have a fixed length of line between the float on the surface and the anchor or weight at the bottom. The length corresponds to the depth of water.

If the buoys are small, they can be carried in the boat or streamed just over the stern with the weights/anchors in the boat.

Take care when driving away not to wrap any of the lines around the propeller.

If the buoys are to be carried in the boat, consider holding each buoy with its ground tackle in separate containers to avoid tangles.

When the desired position is reached, simply drop the weight/anchor over the side of the safety boat and the buoy should remain where it is left.

Recovering the mark

Pick up the buoy in exactly the same way as picking up a mooring. Gather up the line and anchor, stowing it as above.

TIDAL LOCATION

Laying the mark

The buoy should have a pulley block at its base, the line fixing its position will run through this block. On one end will be an anchor or heavy weight, (the buoy may have to sit in a strong tidal stream so this weight/anchor may be substantial), a lighter counter-weight goes on the other end. The length of line used should be the maximum depth of water expected on the day, plus one third.

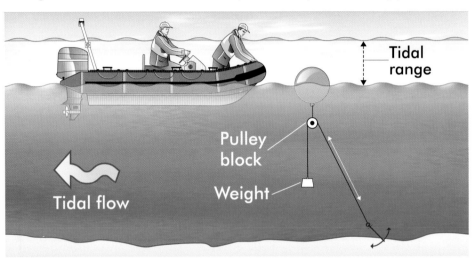

- The anchor for the marker buoy should be placed and tethered into the stern of the safety boat. The counter-weight and buoy can be dropped over the stern.

- Drive away carefully and slowly, so as not to entangle the line in the propeller, paying out the remaining line. The buoy will stream out until it is stopped by the counter-weight.

- When the desired position is reached, the boat should be carefully brought to a halt. This will cause the counter-weight to sink and as it does so, the buoy will be drawn towards the safety boat.

- Drop the primary anchor over the stern of the safety boat.

- The buoy is now fixed in position, and the pulley system will allow for any rise and fall of the tide.

🔄 Recovery

- Pick up the marker buoy in exactly the same way as picking up a mooring.

- Recover the anchor line. (This should be the one that is stretching away and out into the tidal stream).

- Place and tether the anchor into the stern well of the safety boat. The counter-weight and buoy can be left in the water.

- Drive away carefully allowing the buoy to stream as described above.

There are two basic methods used for towing, towing astern and towing along side.

TOWING ASTERN

The advantages of this method are:	The disadvantages are:
• it is quick to organise. • requires only one line. • the two vessels are well apart from each other. • the tow can be 'ditched' quickly.	• there is little control over the towed vessel unless steered. • In a large sea, there can be considerable 'snatch' from the towline, therefore care must be used when choosing the strong points on both vessels before the tow begins.

 Towing a single vessel

Prepare the towline on the safety boat, preferably spreading the load between two points if possible. A bridle on the transom is the best method for this.

Approach the vessel to be towed, usually from downwind, towards its bow and pass the towline to the other vessel. Make the line fast to the painter, or through a fairlead and around the mast of a dinghy.

Centralise the steering and raise the centre-board of a dinghy. Move the crew to the back of the boat to trim the bow up.

Gently motor away and take up the slack in the towline.

Ease back on the power as the load comes onto the towline.

Motor gently back to safety, monitoring the towed vessel regularly.

If the rescued vessel is to be put onto a mooring, consider picking up the mooring with the safety boat first, then pulling up the rescued vessel afterwards. If the rescued vessel has to be brought alongside a berth, then consider towing alongside for better control. If towing astern at speed, be careful to adjust the length of the warp so that the tow is able to ride your wake, rather than 'digging in.'

Towing a string of dinghies

Again, there are two basic methods. Dinghies under tow should be trimmed with the weight aft and centreboards raised or nearly raised so that they track properly.

Chained or in-line tow

The disadvantage is that there is a greater strain on the first boats in the tow.

This works well in light conditions. Fasten each dinghy painter to the boat in front – usually to the toe straps. Centreboards should be raised or nearly raised and only the last boat in the chain should be steered, with its rudder down.

Herringbone tow

The tug streams a long warp, possibly with loops or stopper knots – though these do tangle. Each dinghy ties in to the warp, using a rolling hitch on a plain warp.

Each boat's painter should ideally be led from the pivot point, (usually the mast), and each boat should be steered with a partially lowered centreboard. It is usually easier to pick up recent arrivals at the head of the tow.

This can be a highly effective means of picking up a fleet prior to towing home, by driving through the fleet trailing the warp, but be careful of tangles from a standing start.

Tug

TOWING ALONGSIDE

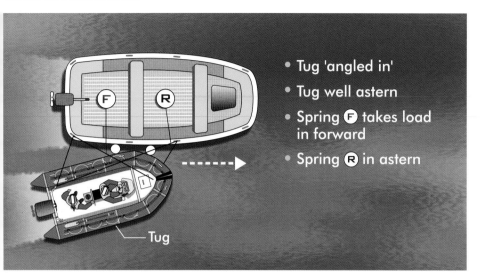

- Tug 'angled in'
- Tug well astern
- Spring **F** takes load in forward
- Spring **R** in astern

Tug

Bring the safety boat alongside the vessel to be towed. Consider using fenders to protect each vessel.

Position the 'tug' so that its rudder/outboard motor is aft of the towed vessel's transom, and bow in towards the tow. You should be able to direct the steering either side of the pivot point of the tow.

Secure bow and stern lines between 'tug' and 'tow' to hold them firmly together.

Take a line from the bow of the safety boat to the stern of the tow. Do the same with a line from the stern of the safety boat to the bow of the tow. These lines are called 'springs' and take the loads when power is applied forward or astern. Ensure all lines are taut before driving off.

This set-up is compact and relatively easy to manoeuvre. It takes time to set up and cast off; since the boats are in contact hard boats will require fendering.

A quick alongside tow of one or two dinghies can be achieved by putting one very tight line round the mast of each dinghy. Be careful to balance the boats and watch your speed.

Top Tip

Towing alongside, it is vital to get all the lines tight – otherwise control is impossible.

APPENDIX 1
EQUIPMENT FOR THE SAFETY BOAT

The general principle is to carry what will be useful at the venue, but nothing which is very unlikely to be used.

Things to consider:

- Is the safety boat operating in isolation or with other boats?
- Is there a 'mother ship' which could carry extra or heavier equipment?
- Is the safety boat operating close to its home base or away from it?
- What sort of boats/sailors are there?
- Is it a coastal or inland venue?
- Is there potential for the activity running on after daylight fades?
- What time of the year is it?

The following equipment list is not definitive, but the answers to the above questions will determine the priorities.

ESSENTIAL AT COASTAL SITES

- Anchor (appropriate to the size of boat and bottom surface), sufficient chain/warp to anchor securely.
- A float/fender for buoying an abandoned anchor.
- Paddles/oars
- Spare fuel
- Towlines x2 (preferably including 1 floating line with snap hooks)
- Flares (appropriate to the operating area)
- Sharp serrated knife
- First aid kit (contents vary depending on the venue/ operating authority).
- Survival bag (preferably big enough for 2 people)
- Spare kill cord

ADDITIONAL ITEMS TO CONSIDER

- VHF
- Bucket/bailer
- Tool/spares bag
- Boarding ladder/recovery cradle
- Throw bag
- Tags or chinagraph pencil ('crew safe')
- Spare anchor and warp
- Spare propeller (and tools to attach it)
- Spare shear pin
- Navigation equipment (coastal venues)
- Remote submersible bilge pump
- Large comprehensive first aid kit
- Blankets/spare clothing
- Hot drinks
- Bolt crops
- Binoculars
- Fire extinguisher

Any equipment that the safety boat does carry must be in serviceable order (waterproofed, if necessary) and stowed securely, but ready for instant use. It can be helpful to label items.

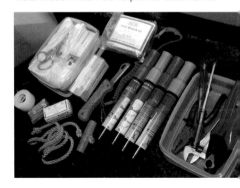

Top tip

See the Guidance Notes for the Inspection of RYA Recognised Training Centres for the minimum equipment requirements for recognised Training Centres.

APPENDIX 2
SAFETY BOAT MAINTENANCE

A well maintained safety boat is reliable and cheaper to run in the long term.

A log of each safety boat's hours and maintenance schedule can be useful: Encourage all operators to report faults and defects as soon as possible.

Fuel storage and handling requires care for safety as well as operational reasons. If you mix two-stroke oil with petrol manually, make the process as simple as possible.

Other regular checks could be split between monthly/weekly and daily checks. The frequency should be decided by the organisation concerned.

Consider an annual service by a qualified service technician. Modern engines have quite sophisticated engine management systems that may require specialist diagnostic equipment.

A good way to ensure that the checks are carried out is to have a check list with space for recording any defects.

Here is a general checklist:

- Check kill cord actually stops the engine.

- Check steering operation is smooth? If not it may only need lubrication. Pay particular attention to hydraulic systems that may develop tiny leaks. If these are not rectified catastrophic steering failure can result.

- Check fuel filters are clean.

- Check oil level on four-stroke engines – do not overfill.

- Is the propeller in good condition? Damaged props cause gearbox problems and excessive vibration.

- Is the gear shift smooth and easy to operate?

- Does the interlock work?

- Is the engine secure?

- Is all safety kit on board and in order?

Safety Boat Handbook

APPENDIX 3
KNOTS FOR THE SAFETY BOAT CREW

Speed of response is important and it is often quicker if no knots have to be tied. Spring gate carbine hooks or karabiners on some of the towlines are worth considering. These can be clipped into loops or strong points, and eliminate worry about whether a knot will hold, or which knot to tie.

Towline with spring hook

There will come a time when knots are necessary. Here is a useful selection:

Bowline: Provides a loop onto which another line can be fastened or to make a line secure. Can be united even if it has been heavily loaded, but not while under load.

Sheet bend: not as secure as a double sheet bend, but quicker to tie.

Double sheet bend: Used commonly to fasten a painter to a towline, but its most common use is to join two lines of different diameter together.

Eye splice: Permanent, strong loop in the end of a laid rope.

Figure of Eight: A simple knot which can have a carbine hook clipped into it. Can be undone after it has had a load placed on it.

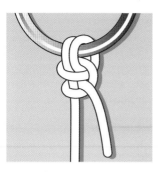

Fisherman's bend: As round turn and two half hitches but more secure. Can jam once loaded.

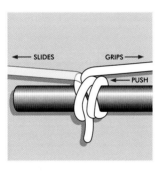
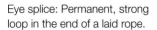

Rolling hitch: Used to attach a line part way down another line, usually for herringbone tows. Only grips in one direction – wind twice down towards the tail of the towline, and capture the turns by going back up once.

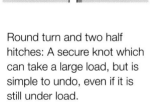

Round turn and two half hitches: A secure knot which can take a large load, but is simple to undo, even if it is still under load.

Common whipping: Used to prevent the end of a laid (3 strand) rope.

The safety boat should be equipped with several towlines (possibly of varying length), coiled and ready to use. A lighter heaving line or a throwbag can be useful as well, in order to get a line to a situation that may be difficult to get alongside. Throwbags pay out floating line when thrown and with practice can be thrown accurately to a small target. Long throws made under pressure often miss!

APPENDIX 4
WHICH TYPE OF SAFETY BOAT?

No one boat will be completely suitable, so a compromise will be necessary. The choice will generally come down to three types, and choosing a boat the following will need to be taken into consideration.

Venue Is the sailing area generally flat, or is it prone to large waves? Will the boats be moored or slipped and kept on a trolley?
Boat types Are they robust craft for beginners or more specialised and fragile?
Monohulls or cats? Cats are fast and may require quicker safety cover.
Students/participants Beginners or experienced?
Type of session Taster sessions or intensive racing requiring big marks to be laid?

RIBs (Rigid Inflatable Boats)

Versatile but expensive, these are probably the most popular choice.

ADVANTAGES	DISADVANTAGES
Inflatable sponsons provide soft contact with other craft.	Vulnerable to damage. The tubes are not fenders.
High buoyancy.	Sometimes require a vehicle to launch and recover.
Most have excellent sea keeping qualities.	
High load carrying capacity with low freeboard.	The sponsons are difficult to anti-foul successfully.
High speeds possible.	Can be prone to UV degradation.
Stable teaching platform.	

Dories and 'Plastic Boats'

Best suited to inland/sheltered locations.

ADVANTAGES

Large load carrying capacity.
Robust.
Stable platform at rest.
Low freeboard good for windsurfing and single-handed dinghies.
Cheap to buy and require a lower powered engine.
Can be beached.
Small ones can be launched and recovered without a vehicle.
Plastic types are very tough.
There are several versions with loading ramps, which can be useful for assisting capsized disabled sailors.

DISADVANTAGES

Hard, uncomfortable ride in waves.
Usually double skinned, so can be difficult to drain/dry out if damaged.
Leaks into the under-floor void can be hard to detect.
Hard sides can cause damage when coming alongside jetties or other vessels.
Can be a 'wet' boat to work in.

Displacement craft

These are well suited to race support, carrying marks and ground tackle, perform ferrying duties and acting as comfortable and visible committee boats. They also make very good tugs, being powerful enough to tow several craft with little loss of performance.

ADVANTAGES

Comfortable at sea.
Provide a dry ride for the crew.
Economical due to the (usual) inboard engine.
Huge load carrying capacity.
Comfortable for the crew at anchor.

DISADVANTAGES

High initial cost.
Not easily launched/recovered or transported by road.
Usually require a mooring or berth.
Slow.
Not very manoeuvrable in a rescue situation.
Should not be beached.
High freeboard hard sides, so limited rescue capability.

Since the final choice is often determined by price, it may sometimes be worth considering the second hand market for the boat hull. Modern outboard engines are reliable and have long warranties from new, so there may be a stronger case for a new engine. It can also be helpful to visit a similar venue to find out what they are using and why. If possible, see the boat in use.

Safety Boat Handbook

APPENDIX 5
STANDARD ADVICE TO SAILORS FOLLOWING A CAPSIZE

The point of no return for this dinghy crew. They are about to capsize during a gybe - probably because the centreboard is too far down, and they did not move their weight to the new windward side quickly enough as the boom swung across.

Capsizing

Knowing how to deal with a capsize is an important part of learning to sail small boats. At a RYA recognised sailing school, you will be taught how to handle a capsize.

Practise capsizing under controlled conditions. In this way you will learn the simple techniques for righting the boat and gain confidence for dealing with the real situation.

How often you have to recover from a capsize will depend on the type of boat you sail, your level of skill, and the conditions you sail in. Racers will tend to push the limits more frequently than cruisers.

Once you have mastered a recovery technique that works well for your type of boat, a capsize will usually be little more than an inconvenience from which you can quickly recover.

Top tip
If you find yourself in the water under a sail just put your hand above your head to create an airspace and swim to the edge of the sail.

Righting a two-person boat

The most common type of capsize occurs when the boat heels too much and capsizes to leeward. This type of capsize is relatively slow and gentle. Your buoyancy aid will keep you afloat so relax:

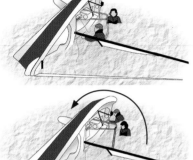

1. As the boat falls onto its side, helmsman and crew lower themselves into the water between the hull and the sail. Both helmsman and crew work their way to the stern and check that the rudder is secure on its fastenings and has not floated off.

2. The helmsman takes the end of the mainsheet as a safety line and swims round the hull to the centreboard. He checks it is fully down; if not the crew puts it down. (If the helmsman is very light, the crew may go to the centreboard.)

3. The crew now moves back into the boat and finds the end of the upper jib sheet, throwing it over the hull to the helmsman.

4. Once he has the jib sheet, the helmsman lets go of the mainsheet and climbs onto the centreboard. The crew floats inside the boat, holding on to a toestrap and checking the mainsheet is free.

5. The helmsman now stands with his feet near the hull and leans back on the jib sheet. The mast and sails will slowly start to lift from the water as the boat comes upright. The crew will be scooped aboard and can help the helmsman into the boat over the side or stern.

Safety Boat Handbook

Top tip

Once modern boats are fully inverted they have no effective air pocket underneath. Stay clear of an inverting boat.

Righting from an inversion

Any boat will turn completely upside down if left on its side for long. This is known as inversion. Some boats are more prone to this than others.

The first step in recovering is to bring the boat back on to its side. Pull yourself onto the upturned hull and stand on the edge while leaning back against the centreboard. If the centreboard has retracted into its case, use a sheet from the other side of the boat to pull against. Now use the standard righting method.

After inversion stand on the edge of the boat and lean back on the centreboard to bring the boat onto its side.

If you have to right an inverted catamaran, sit on the stern of the leeward hull until the opposite bow lifts and the mast starts to come to the surface. As it does so, move to the middle of the lower hull and continue the normal righting process.

Righting a singlehander

Righting a singlehander is easy if you can climb over the high side and onto the centreboard as the boat goes over. From here you can quickly pull the boat upright and climb aboard – staying dry throughout the process. If you fail to climb over the high side or if the boat capsizes to windward, lower yourself gently into the water. Use the mainsheet as a safety line and swim round the hull to the centreboard. To right the boat, pull on the centreboard, or climb onto it. As you pull on the side of the hull the boat will right itself and you can climb aboard.

Top tip

Many boats will drift faster when on their side than you can swim so always keep hold of the boat when you are in the water.

Righting a catamaran

As the catamaran capsizes, slide into the water between the trampoline and the sail. Keep hold of something – the boat may drift quite fast. Once capsized a catamaran can be harder to right than a dinghy, especially if it turns upside down.

1. Move around the front beam to the underside of the boat. Climb onto the hull and throw the righting line over the upper hull. Free the sheets and traveller to prevent the boat sailing away once righted.

2. Turn the boat so that the mast points into wind (the opposite to a dinghy) – the windage of the trampoline and rig will help you right the boat. If necessary, gently depress the bow to swing the hulls around in the breeze.

3. Lean back on the righting line (or sheet) to lift the mast tip clear of the water. When the mast lifts clear, the wind will get under the sail, lifting it. The boat will start to right more quickly.

4. Stay under the boat by the front beam as the top hull drops back into the water. Be careful it does not hit you. Grab the front beam as it comes down. This will prevent the boat sailing off or capsizing again.

5. Climb aboard over either beam, check the rudder and sheets and stow any loose lines. Climbing over the lower rear beam is easier if you are tired.

GLOSSARY

Asymmetric (1)	Spinnaker-type sail rigged from front of extending pole
Asymmetric (2 Abbrev)	Boat with asymmetric spinnaker.
Boom	Metal or wooden spar along bottom of sail
Cat (Abbrev.)	Catamaran, fast boat with two hulls
Cunningham	See Downhaul
Downhaul	Pulley system for tensioning leading edge of sail
DSC	Digital Selective Calling
Forestay	Wire from high up mast to bow, usually attached to jib
Inversion	Capsize completely so the rig points downwards
Jason's Cradle	Roll-up system for recovering people from the water
Jib	Small sail at front of boat
Kicker	Pulley system between base of mast and boom
Kill cord	Clip which stops engine when detached
Kite	See spinnaker
Leach	Trailing edge of sail
Luff	Leading edge of sail
Main or Mainsail	Big sail on dinghy, with front edge (luff) attached to mast
Painter	Rope attached to front of boat
Port	Left side of boat, as seen facing forwards
RIB	Rigid Inflatable Boat
Sheet	Rope for controlling sail
Spinnaker	Big balloon sail at front of boat, used sailing downwind
Sponson	Inflatable tube around sides of RIB
Spring	Rope rigged to take fore-and aft-loads.
Starboard	Right side of boat, as seen facing forwards
Traveller	Track across boat enabling sails to be trimmed at different angles
Turtle	See inversion
Universal joint	Flexible connection between windsurfer rig and board
Warp	Rope used to tow or tie up a vessel
Wishbone	Used to control windsurfer sail

BIBLIOGRAPHY

RYA Start Powerboating G48
RYA Powerboat Handbook G13
RYA Powerboat Logbook G20
First Aid Manual ZF03
RYA VHF Radio including GMDSS G22
RYA VHF Handbook G31

INDEX

INDEX

Safety Boat Handbook

RYA *Membership*

Promoting and Protecting Boating
www.rya.org.uk

RYA Membership

Promoting and Protecting Boating

The RYA is the national organisation which represents the interests of everyone who goes boating for pleasure.

The greater the membership, the louder our voice when it comes to protecting members' interests.

Apply for membership today, and support the RYA, to help the RYA support you.

Benefits of Membership

- Access to expert advice on all aspects of boating from legal wrangles to training matters
- Special members' discounts on a range of products and services including boat insurance, books, videos and class certificates
- Free issue of certificates of competence, increasingly asked for by everyone from overseas governments to holiday companies, insurance underwriters to boat hirers

- Access to the wide range of RYA publications, including the quarterly magazine
- Third Party insurance for windsurfing members
- Free Internet access with RYA-Online
- Special discounts on AA membership
- Regular offers in RYA Magazine
- ...and much more

Join now - membership form opposite

Join online at *www.rya.org.uk*

Visit our website for information, advice, members' services and web shop.

1 **Important** To help us comply with Data Protection legislation, please tick *either* Box A or Box B (you must tick Box A to ensure you receive the full benefits of RYA membership). The RYA will not pass your data to third parties.

☐ **A.** I wish to join the RYA and receive future information on member services, benefits (as listed in RYA Magazine and website) and offers.

☐ **B.** I wish to join the RYA but do not wish to receive future information on member services, benefits (as listed in RYA Magazine and website) and offers.

When completed, please send this form to: RYA, RYA House, Ensign Way, Hamble, Southampton, SO31 4YA

2

Title	Forename	Surname	Date of Birth		Male	Female
			DD / MM / YY		☐	☐
1.						
2.			DD / MM / YY		☐	☐
3.			DD / MM / YY		☐	☐
4.			DD / MM / YY		☐	☐

Address

Town   County   Post Code

Evening Telephone   Daytime Telephone

email

Signature: Date:

3 **Type of membership required:** *(Tick Box)*

☐ **Personal** Annual rate £37 or £34 by Direct Debit
From 1st October 2007 annual rate £39 or £36 by Direct Debit

☐ **Under 21** Annual rate £12 (no reduction for Direct Debit)
From 1st October 2007 will be £13

☐ **Family*** Annual rate £56 or £52 by Direct Debit
From 1st October 2007 annual rate £58 or £54 by Direct Debit

* Family Membership: 2 adults plus any under 21s all living at the same address

4 Please tick ONE box to show your main boating interest.

☐ Yacht Racing	☐ Yacht Cruising
☐ Dinghy Racing	☐ Dinghy Cruising
☐ Personal Watercraft	☐ Inland Waterways
☐ Powerboat Racing	☐ Windsurfing
☐ Motor Boating	☐ Sportsboats and RIBs

Please see Direct Debit form overleaf

![RYA logo]

Instructions to your Bank or Building Society to pay by Direct Debit

Please complete this form and return it to:
Royal Yachting Association, RYA House, Ensign Way, Hamble, Southampton, Hampshire SO31 4YA

DIRECT Debit

Originators Identification Number

9	5	5	2	1	3

To The Manager: _____ Bank/Building Society

Address: _____

Post Code: _____

2. Name(s) of account holder(s)

_____

3. Branch Sort Code

		—			—		

4. Bank or Building Society account number

Banks and Building Societies may not accept Direct Debit instructions for some types of account

5. RYA Membership Number (For office use only)

6. Instruction to pay your Bank or Building Society

Please pay Royal Yachting Association Direct Debits from the account detailed in this instruction subject to the safeguards assured by The Direct Debit Guarantee.
I understand that this instruction may remain with the Royal Yachting Association and, if so, details will be passed electronically to my Bank/Building Society.

Signature(s) _____

Date _____

Office use / Centre Stamp

Cash, Cheque, Postal Order enclosed £ _____
Made payable to the Royal Yachting Association

Office use only: Membership Number Allocated

077